GLOW IN THE DARK:
VOYAGE THROUGH
SPACE

written by
KATY FLINT

illustrated by
CORNELIA LI

WIDE EYED EDITIONS

At its center, the Sun is 27 million degrees Fahrenheit.

SUNSPOTS are cooler, darker-looking patches on the Sun's surface.

SOLAR FLARES are explosions that come out from the surface of the Sun.

1.3 million Earths could fit inside the Sun.

The Sun isn't special—there are many, many other stars just like it in space. But to us it's the most important star in the universe, because without it, there would be no life on Earth.

THE SUN

Our adventure begins at the very center of our solar system. The Sun is a star that gives off light and heat. Its pulling force, called gravity, keeps our solar system together. On our journey, we will visit the eight planets that travel around the Sun in oval paths, called orbits. The closest four planets to the Sun are made of rock. We could stand on them if we had the right space suit to protect us from the Sun's heat and to help us breathe. The next four planets are much larger and made of gas. They don't have solid surfaces, so we would fall through them if we tried to land. Let's explore! Watch out for explosions, asteroids, and comets on our VOYAGE THROUGH SPACE!

The solar system is part of our galaxy, a big group of stars, called THE MILKY WAY. There are billions of galaxies in the universe.

MERCURY

Mercury is the first stop on our journey and the closest planet to the Sun. It is the smallest planet in our solar system and moves around the Sun very quickly. Look around! Mercury's wrinkled gray surface is scarred with craters. Meteors have been crashing into it for millions of years. In fact, it looks very much like Earth's moon. Scorched by solar rays, this planet is blisteringly hot in the daytime and very cold at night.

Mercury is the closest planet to the Sun.

Mercury does not have a moon. A moon is an object that makes an orbit around a planet.

Most planets are named after Roman gods and goddesses. Mercury is named after the winged messenger god because it moves around the Sun so quickly.

The Sun looks huge in the sky because Mercury is so close to it.

A robotic probe called MESSENGER orbited Mercury hundreds of times to take pictures of the planet and beam information back to Earth.

A year is the time it takes a planet to go around the Sun. On Earth, a year is 365.25 days, whereas on Mercury, a year is only 88 days long.

Japan's AKATSUKI spacecraft has completed successful orbits around Venus. It was sent there to learn about the planet's toxic atmosphere, cloud layers, volcanoes, and lightning.

Venus is the second planet from the Sun and Earth's closest neighbor.

Temperatures can reach a sizzling 860 degrees Fahrenheit on Venus.

Without the right equipment, life on Venus would be very short. On stepping out of the spacecraft, you'd be squashed flat by pressure and fried by heat. This is before you'd even had a chance to breathe in the poisonous gases!

Venus does not have a moon.

VENUS

Next is Venus, the hottest planet in our solar system. It is covered with thick clouds that bounce and scatter sunlight into space. If you were to stand on the planet's gray rocks, everything would look orange due to the way light filters through the thick atmosphere. This atmosphere acts like a blanket and traps the Sun's heat, making Venus violently hot. Crippling pressure, acid rain, intense heat, lightning storms, and hurricane winds make this planet impossible to explore... for now.

Stepping down onto the moon, we can look back on Earth in the distance. Earth is our home planet and has just the right conditions for life to exist. It is not too hot, or too cold, and it is covered in water. Because there is so much water, life has developed there. Full of mountains, greenery, and oceans, Earth is home to millions of plants and animals. The moon looks dusty, rocky, and gray in comparison. We've not found anywhere else in the universe with the same conditions as Earth...So let's keep exploring!

MOON

There was a space race between the U.S.A. and the U.S.S.R. to send the first humans to the moon. In 1969, American astronauts Neil Armstrong and Buzz Aldrin were the first to touch down here.

Footprints stay on the moon for millions of years because there isn't any wind or rain to get rid of them.

One side of the moon always faces away from Earth, so you can never see it. This is called the "far side of the moon."

Earth is the third planet from the Sun.

EARTH

Earth is the only planet in our solar system to have just one moon. Some have many, and others have none.

Scientists at the National Aeronautics and Space Administration (NASA), helped to get astronauts to the moon. They calculated detailed paths for takeoff and landing—making sure the astronauts could get home safe.

EARTH AND MOON

MARS

Be sure to spot the two moons, DEIMOS and PHOBOS, while you're here.

Mars is the fourth planet from the Sun.

Mars is home to the largest volcano in our solar system— OLYMPUS MONS.

The dry surface of Mars is rocky and full of craters.

Mars is named after the Roman god of war.

Next stop Mars: the rusty red planet. Don't be fooled by the fiery red color, the temperature on Mars can be extremely cold—as low as minus 150 degrees Fahrenheit at night. But like Earth, Mars has seasons, and on a Martian summer's day, the temperature can reach 68 degrees Fahrenheit. However, the winds can be fierce all year round, wearing down rocks and whipping dust into clouds that turn the sky pink. A dust storm is coming...We better go!

One Martian day is called a "sol" and is roughly 39 minutes longer than a day on Earth. A day on Earth is 24 hours long.

Dust Storm

We think Mars was once more like Earth. It had rivers, lakes, and volcanoes. But Mars dried up and cooled down, while Earth developed the conditions for life to grow.

CERES is the largest object in the asteroid belt, and it is called a DWARF PLANET. Dwarf planets are round and orbit the Sun.

Asteroids are made out of rock, metal, or both.

Sometimes asteroids can fall to Earth, although they normally burn up before they get there. If they reach Earth, we call them meteorites.

THE ASTEROID BELT

CERES

The word "asteroid" means "star-like."

We've arrived at the asteroid belt between Mars and Jupiter! Asteroids are pieces of rock that orbit the Sun, but they are too small and misshapen to be called planets. They are all different shapes and sizes—some are as small as 30 feet, and some are as large as 300 miles wide! There are millions of asteroids here, but don't worry, we won't crash into them, as they are far apart. Billions of years ago, as the solar system developed, the whole universe looked like the asteroid belt. Scientists think that asteroids joined together to form the planets.

Scientists think a large meteor strike caused the extinction of the dinosaurs. The asteroid that fell to Earth was about 6 miles wide and caused earthquakes, fires, tidal waves, and volcanic eruptions.

Every day on Jupiter is cloudy. But it has lightning storms brighter than any on Earth.

Fly to Jupiter's north pole to see a light show called an aurora.

CALLISTO

We haven't found life anywhere else in the universe yet, but it might exist here!

EUROPA

Jupiter's four largest moons are named GANYMEDE, CALLISTO, IO, and EUROPA—but it has many others. Explosive Io is covered with volcanoes and pizza-colored markings, while icy Europa is thought to have water beneath its surface.

JUPITER

Stormy Jupiter is the largest planet in our solar system. This king of the planets is covered with multicolored stripes and spots...but there is one very angry red spot that stands out from the rest. The Great Red Spot is a huge storm, bigger than Earth itself, which has been raging for hundreds of years. As we get close to Jupiter's stripes, we can see and smell that they are fast-moving clouds of poisonous gases. We'll stop before we get too close. If we flew through the layers of cloud to its liquid surface, we wouldn't survive.

IO

GANYMEDE

Great Red Spot

NASA's JUNO spacecraft is studying Jupiter at the moment.

Jupiter is the fifth planet from the Sun.

SATURN

At Saturn's north pole is a storm shaped like a hexagon. There's nothing like it in the rest of the solar system.

Look out for Saturn's moons—especially ENCELADUS. It is one of the brightest objects in space.

Saturn is the sixth planet from the Sun.

NASA's CASSINI spacecraft traveled to Saturn to gather new information. It sent back amazing pictures of Saturn's rings and moons.

A year on Saturn is more than 29 Earth years.

Saturn, the ringed planet, is our next destination. Its rings are made of very small bits of ice, dust, and rock that circle around the planet. Many moons are scattered between its rings and beyond. Living on Saturn would be impossible, as its surface is made mostly of swirling gases and liquids. But a few of its moons, such as Enceladus, are thought to have their own oceans. So one day, life could be possible there!

You can see Saturn glowing gold in the night sky from Earth.

The weather on Saturn is more windy than the very strongest hurricanes on Earth.

URANUS

Uranus has 13 faint rings but they are not as bright and shiny as Saturn's.

Uranus has 27 moons named after famous characters from Shakespeare plays.

Uranus is the seventh planet from the Sun.

Uranus is named after the Greek god of the sky. It is the only planet to be named after a Greek god rather than a Roman god.

NASA'S VOYAGER 2 is the only probe to explore all four gas giants.

As we leave Saturn, look out for Uranus, glowing blue in the distance. Uranus spins on its side, and looks like it has been knocked over. It has the coldest surface in the universe and we cannot stand on it, as it is another gas planet. Beneath its blue-green clouds, scientists think diamonds fall like hailstones. Mountains of gems are pulled toward the planet's core and form shimmering oceans, where massive gems float like icebergs. If only we could get down there to check...

Because of the way Uranus spins, one side of the planet faces the Sun for a very long time, and then faces away from it for a very long time.

The largest storm on Neptune was spotted by Voyager 2 and named the "Great Dark Spot." It has since disappeared, so maybe it's over!

The final planet on our journey is Neptune, the ice giant. It is thought to be the windiest planet in our solar system—even windier than its fellow gas giant Jupiter. It looks deep blue because of the methane gas in its atmosphere. Bright white clouds streak across this planet, and one moves very quickly indeed—it's nicknamed "scooter." Neptune is the farthest planet from the Sun, and there's lots we still don't know about it.

Neptune is the eighth planet from the Sun.

This planet goes around the Sun once every 165 Earth years.

NEPTUNE

Six faint rings circle the planet

It took 12 years for VOYAGER 2 to reach Neptune from Earth.

Scooter

TRITON

There are 13 moons that have been discovered so far orbiting Neptune.

Neptune's largest moon, TRITON, has ice volcanoes. It's extremely cold at minus 390 degrees Fahrenheit, and its frosty surface has the texture of a cantaloupe.

CHARON

PLUTO

Pluto has five moons.
Its closest moon is
called CHARON.

Pluto has a heart-
shaped marking on its
surface.

In the Kuiper belt, we find
Pluto. Pluto used to be called
a planet, but astronomers
now call it a dwarf planet, like
Ceres. It is so small it could fit
inside the United States.

Most comets begin life in
the Kuiper belt as chunks
of rock and ice. As they
speed toward the Sun,
they heat up, leaving an
icy trail behind them.

THE KUIPER BELT

We have now traveled billions of miles from the Sun and have reached the Kuiper belt. It is very much like the asteroid belt, but 200 times bigger and 20 times wider. This frisbee-shaped area is made up of thousands of lumps of ice, rock, and metal, which orbit the Sun very slowly. Past the edges of our solar system lurks interstellar space. Only one spacecraft has ever gone this far before, NASA's Voyager 1. It's time for us to return home and plan our next adventure...

NASA's NEW HORIZONS spacecraft has been exploring Pluto and its moons.

Glow in the Dark: Voyage Through Space © 2018 Quarto Publishing plc.
Illustrations by Cornelia Li. Written by Katy Flint.
Consultant Ed Bloomer, Astronomer, Royal Observatory Greenwich.

First Published in 2018 by Wide Eyed Editions, an imprint of The Quarto Group.
400 First Avenue North, Suite 400, Minneapolis, MN 55401, USA.
T (612) 344-8100 F (612) 344-8692 **www.QuartoKnows.com**

ISBN 978-1-78603-131-0

The illustrations were created digitally using hand-painted textures.
Set in Hipton Sans, Roboto Slab, and Apercu.

Published by Jenny Broom
Designed by Nicola Price
Production by Catherine Cragg
Manufactured in Guangdong, China CC042018
9 8 7 6 5 4 3 2 1

melbourne

victoria . australia

a photographic essay. peter emanuel's
impressions of melbourne, victoria.
thankyou God for your creation

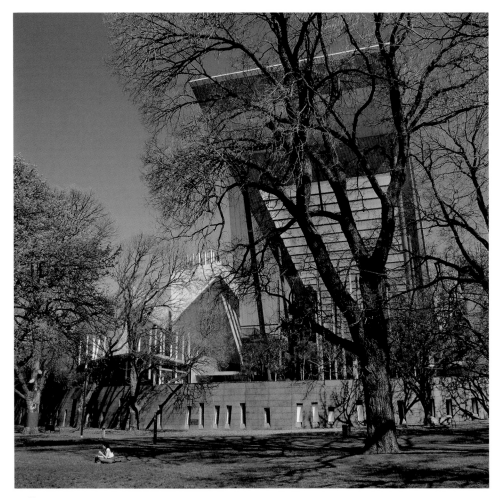

8   exhibition buildings and melbourne museum

a. st pauls cathedral b. queen victoria gardens c. treasury gardens d. sidney myer music bowl
e. parliament f. st kilda rd g. st patricks cathedral h. polly woodside i. government house

12   shrine of remembrance and the city

melbourne convention centre and crown entertainment complex on either side of the yarra   13

16   a. sandringham yacht club b. station pier c. swanson dock

a. st kilda beach b. kings domain c. albert park   17

18   city skyline

a. sandringham yacht club b. brighton baths c. brighton beach d. catani gardens, st kilda 19
e & f. south melbourne g h & i. royal melbourne golf club

20   collins street east

next page. st pauls cathedral and flinders street station

a b c f h & i. collins street. d & e. gordon reserve 21

24   st patricks cathedral

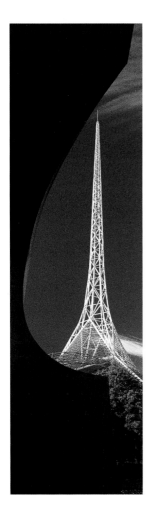
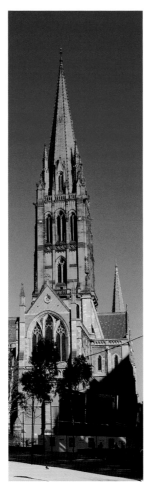

a. arts centre spire   b. st pauls cathedral   c. rialto towers   25

26   a&f. st pauls cathedral b. state library c&i. rmit d. swanston street e. matthew flinders statue g. town hall h. lamp post detail

next page. federation square with flinders street station and st pauls cathedral.

34   moomba parade

40   a. melbourne park b. melbourne sports & aquatic centre c. tennis centre

next page. melbourne cricket ground

australian rules football 43

46   docklands stadium

next page. speigel tent, arts centre forecourt

58   queen victoria market

next page. federation square and city reflections

a. alexandra gardens b & c. queen victoria gardens 69

federation bells   83

88   a. port phillip bay b. brighton yatch club c. brighton baths

90   brighton bathing boxes

next page. brighton beach bathing boxes and city

st kilda pier   91

melbourne city skyline   95

visit the peter emanuel galleries on line www.peteremanuel.com.au